Original Title: Samurai Legacy

© Samurai Legacy, Carlos Martínez Cerdá and Víctor Martínez Cerdá, 2023

Authors: Víctor Martínez Cerdá and Carlos Martínez Cerdá (V&C Brothers)

© Cover and illustrations: V&C Brothers

Layout and design: V&C Brothers

SAMURAI LEGACY

LEGENDS, MYSTERIES, AND CURIOSITIES

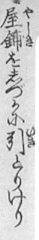

1

The word "samurai" originates from Japan and refers to a warrior class that existed in the country for several centuries.

The word itself comes from the Japanese verb "saburau," which means "to serve," so samurais were considered warriors who served their feudal lord, the daimyo, with the mission of protecting him.

The emergence of the samurai class dates back to the Heian period in Japan (794-1185), when groups of armed warriors were formed to protect the nobles and the imperial court.

However, it was during the Japanese feudal period (1185-1868) that the samurais reached their greatest relevance and influence in Japanese society.

During this period, samurais were hired by feudal lords to protect their territories and serve as administrators and judges.

Samurais were obliged to follow a code of honor and ethics known as "bushido," which established a series of values and principles to which they had to adhere, such as loyalty, courage, and honesty.

Samurais also stood out for their skill in martial arts, and they trained in different combat techniques, such as kenjutsu (the art of the sword) and kyudo (archery).

In addition, samurai culture valued poetry, literature, and music, and many samurais were known for their skills in these areas.

With the arrival of the Meiji era in Japan in 1868, the feudal system was abolished, and the samurais lost their privileged status.

Many samurais became government officials or businessmen, while others dedicated themselves to the arts and letters.

Although the samurai class no longer exists in Japan today, its legacy and influence remain significant in Japanese culture.

2

The figure of the samurai emerged in Japan in the 10th century, but it was from the end of the 12th century that they gained fame and power in Japanese society.

This was largely due to the Genpei Wars, a civil conflict that pitted the Taira and Minamoto clans against each other for control of the Japanese government.

The war began in 1180 and lasted five years, during which several decisive battles were fought.

Finally, in 1185, the Minamoto, led by Minamoto no Yoritomo, defeated the Taira in the Battle of Dan-no-ura and established the first shogunate of Japan.

The shogunate was a military government that effectively had more power than the Emperor himself.

The shoguns were military leaders who ruled Japan in the name of the Emperor, but in practice, they had absolute control over the country.

The samurais were the warrior class that served the shoguns, and they became an important political and social force in feudal Japan.

The samurais were noted for their loyalty, discipline, and skill in martial arts.

They also followed a strict code of honor known as "bushido," which established a series of values and principles they had to adhere to, such as loyalty, courage, and honesty.

The power of the samurais and the shogunate came to an end in the Meiji era, in the mid-19th century, when Japan began a process of modernization and Westernization.

The shogunate was abolished, and the samurais lost their privileged status.

However, their legacy and influence in Japanese culture endure to this day.

3

Samurais followed a strict code of moral and ethical norms known as "bushido," which means "the way of the warrior."

This code was a guide for samurai behavior and was based on seven main virtues: justice, courage, benevolence, courtesy, honesty, honor, and loyalty.

Justice referred to the duty to protect the weak and oppressed, while courage involved facing danger and adversity without fear.

Benevolence required samurais to be compassionate and assist others.

Courtesy focused on respect and consideration for others, while honesty required sincerity and transparency in all actions.

Honor and loyalty were the fundamental pillars of bushido, as a samurai had to defend his honor and fulfill his duty at all times.

If a samurai failed and strayed from this "path," they were considered dishonored and therefore had to commit seppuku, also known as harakiri.

This was a ritual form of suicide in which the samurai opened his abdomen with a dagger, following a carefully established procedure.

This act was considered an atonement for the committed fault and a way to regain lost honor.

It is important to note that bushido was not a static and immutable code of conduct, but evolved over time and with historical and cultural circumstances.

However, its influence on Japanese culture and society has been profound and continues to this day.

4

Harakiri was a common practice among disgraced samurais or those who had made serious mistakes.

The term "harakiri" is a Japanese word meaning "cutting the stomach" and refers to the act of committing ritual suicide by self-inflicting an opening of the abdomen with a tanto, a short knife.

The purpose of harakiri was to regain the honor and dignity that the samurai had lost, as disgrace was considered a great shame in Japanese culture.

The ritual was usually performed in public and followed an established procedure.

Before starting the ritual, the samurai purified himself with a bath and dressed in his best clothes.

Then, he sat on a tatami mat in front of a tray with the tanto and a paper on which he wrote a poem or a letter to express his final feelings.

Afterward, the samurai handed his sword to an assistant and knelt on a special cushion called "seiza."

Then, the samurai took out the tanto and placed it in front of him.

After a few moments of meditation, the samurai stabbed himself in the stomach and made a cut from left to right, followed by a cut from top to bottom.

The assistant would then decapitate the samurai in a single stroke to end his suffering.

Harakiri was a very serious practice and was considered a way to regain lost honor.

Although it is no longer practiced today, the ritual of harakiri remains a part of Japanese culture and history and is a testament to the strong influence of bushido on Japanese society and culture.

5

In addition to the katana, samurais also mastered other weapons, such as the tanto, a type of short knife; the wakizashi, a shorter sword than the katana; the bokken, a wooden sword used for training; the yari, a spear; and the daikyu, a long bow used for war and hunting.

Samurais were also experts in martial arts, such as jujutsu and kendo, and practiced meditation and other disciplines to improve their concentration and self-control.

Samurais served feudal lords known as daimyos and played a significant role in politics and warfare for many centuries.

However, their influence declined as Japan modernized and adopted a centralized government during the Meiji era in the 19th century.

Even so, samurais continue to be an important symbol of Japanese culture and history.

6

The samurai armor was a key element for protection during battle and was designed to cover the entire body of the warrior.

The armor consisted of multiple pieces that fit the samurai's body, allowing great freedom of movement.

The kabuto was the helmet that protected the samurai's head. It was made of iron and had a crest on the top that often took the shape of an animal, a flower, or a particular ornament.

It also had a visor to protect the warrior's face.

The menpo was a facial mask that protected the samurai's face. It was often made of iron and had an opening at the mouth so the samurai could breathe easily.

The armor itself was composed of several pieces, including the dō (chest armor), kusazuri (hip protection), sode (shoulder protection), kote (arm protection), haidate (thigh protection), and suneate (shin protection).

The quality and craftsmanship of the armor varied according to the wealth and importance of the samurai.

The most important and wealthy samurais often wore very detailed and heavy armors, decorated with gold and silver ornaments and other precious materials.

Overall, the samurai armor was a fundamental piece of equipment for the warriors and a symbol of their status and skill on the battlefield.

Today, samurai armor has become an object of great historical and cultural value and can be found in museums and private collections around the world.

7

Samurais burned incense inside their masks before battles.

This was because incense was considered a symbol of purification in Japanese culture, and it was believed to have the power to ward off evil spirits and purify the warrior's soul.

Additionally, it is said that samurais burned incense in their masks in case they were beheaded during battle.

The idea was that the incense smoke would cover the smell of blood and prevent their souls from being tainted on their journey to the afterlife.

It is said that the first samurai to burn incense inside his mask before battle was Kimura Shigenari, a 16th-century warrior known for his bravery and skill on the battlefield.

8

Samurais were known for being skilled and brave warriors, but they were also very cultured and sophisticated individuals.

In addition to their training in martial arts and warfare, samurais also dedicated themselves to learning and perfecting a wide variety of skills and arts.

A samurai's education included the study of literature, poetry, calligraphy, music, meditation, and other arts.

Practicing these skills not only allowed them to develop their knowledge and abilities but also fostered introspection and reflection, which helped samurais to be more balanced and focused on the battlefield.

After the shogunate period came to an end in Japan, many samurais found themselves without work.

However, thanks to their skills and education, many were able to find employment in the public sector, holding important administrative positions in the new Japanese government.

In many cases, their knowledge and skills in traditional Japanese culture and arts were highly valued, allowing them to maintain an influential position in Japanese society.

9

Ronin were samurais who were not affiliated with any particular daimyo or feudal lord.

These warriors could become ronin for various reasons, such as having lost their feudal lord in battle, being expelled from their clan, or simply having retired from active service.

Without a fixed allegiance to any feudal lord, ronin often found themselves in a difficult situation, as they lacked a stable source of income or protection.

However, some ronin became mercenaries or accepted temporary jobs to survive.

The most famous legend about ronin is that of the 47 Ronin, also known as the revenge of the 47 Ronin.

In this story, a group of ronin samurais seeks to avenge the death of their feudal lord, who was forced to commit seppuku or ritual suicide, after being offended by a government official.

The 47 ronin carefully planned their revenge over several years and ultimately achieved their goal, before surrendering to the authorities and facing their punishment.

The story of the 47 Ronin has been the subject of many works of art, including plays, novels, films, and television shows, and has been an example of loyalty and honor in Japanese culture for centuries.

10

Yasuke was an African samurai, known as the "Black Samurai," who lived in 16th century Japan.

According to some theories, Yasuke might have been a slave of the Portuguese Jesuits and arrived in Japan with them.

Other theories suggest he could have been a mercenary or a sailor on a Portuguese ship.

When Yasuke arrived at the court of the daimyo Oda Nobunaga, the powerful feudal lord was impressed by his great stature and dark complexion, and decided to make him part of his court and personal guard.

Yasuke quickly gained Nobunaga's respect and loyalty and became his trusted samurai and advisor.

It is said that Yasuke was trained in the arts of samurai combat and participated in several battles alongside Nobunaga.

However, after Nobunaga's death in 1582, Yasuke disappeared from recorded history, and his ultimate fate remains unknown.

Although Yasuke's story is not widely known, his figure has been the subject of many works of fiction and comics in Japan, and he has been an example of African presence in Japanese history and culture.

11

Western samurais were foreigners who, like Yasuke, arrived in Japan during the Sengoku period (1467-1603) and participated in samurai culture.

Among them are William Adams and Edward Schnell.

William Adams was an English navigator and merchant who arrived in Japan in 1600, after being shipwrecked off the coast of Kyushu.

He was the first Englishman to reach Japan and became an advisor to Tokugawa Ieyasu, the founder of the Tokugawa shogunate.

Adams helped Ieyasu build ships and establish trade relations with England and Holland.

In return, he received lands and became the first Western samurai, adopting the name Miura Anjin. Adams died in Japan in 1620.

Edward Schnell was a German physician who arrived in Japan in 1861, during the Meiji era (1868-1912).

He was hired as the personal physician of the daimyo of Satsuma, and later became the personal physician of Emperor Meiji.

Schnell learned martial arts and became a samurai, adopting the name Ishinosuke.

He also taught Western medicine in Japan and founded a medical school in Kagoshima.

Schnell returned to Germany in 1876, but left a significant mark on the history of medicine and samurai culture in Japan.

12

The social position of a samurai was hereditary, and only the sons of samurais could aspire to become samurais themselves.

This restriction was maintained throughout much of feudal Japan's history, although there were some exceptions.

For example, on some occasions, feudal lords (daimyos) could grant samurai status to an exceptionally talented commoner, as was the case with some martial artists or military strategists.

However, in general, social mobility was very limited in the Japanese feudal system, and most people were born and died in the same social position as their parents.

Additionally, being a samurai meant not only having a privileged position but also entailed certain responsibilities and duties, such as defending their feudal lord and family, maintaining discipline and loyalty, and following a strict code of conduct known as bushido.

13

There were female warriors in Japan, but they were not part of the samurai system.

The onna-bugeisha were noblewomen or women of the warrior class who engaged in military training and defended their homes and families in times of conflict.

Unlike the samurais, they did not have a formal code of conduct and were not considered a social class in themselves.

In addition to the naginata, they also used other weapons like the kaiken (a short knife) and the yumi (a long bow).

Regarding seppuku, this practice was also performed by samurai women and was carried out by making a cut in the abdomen, not the neck.

However, the way it was performed varied depending on the era and historical context.

14

The Meiji era in Japan began in 1868 and was characterized by a period of modernization and Westernization of the country.

The feudal system that had kept the samurais in power for centuries was abolished, and a new national army based on conscription was created.

As a result, the samurai class lost much of its power and political and military influence.

Many samurais became soldiers and officers in the new army, while others turned to civilian jobs such as agriculture or commerce.

Although the term "samurai" continued to be used in Japanese popular culture, the figure of the samurai warriors as they were previously known disappeared with the end of the feudal system.

15

The distinction between samurais and ninjas was not always clear in history.

Both were experts in martial arts and military strategy, and some samurais even became ninjas or hired ninjas in times of need.

However, there are some key differences in how they operated.

Samurais focused on hand-to-hand combat with traditional weapons such as the sword, while ninjas specialized in espionage, infiltration, and assassination using techniques of camouflage, ambushes, and weapons like the shuriken (throwing stars) and the kunai (throwing knife).

Moreover, while samurais were closely associated with feudal lords and the Japanese feudal system, ninjas were more independent and often worked for different clients, including sometimes rival feudal lords.

16

At its peak, the number of samurais in Japan was significant, although there is no exact figure indicating how many samurais there were in total in the country.

During the Edo period, which spanned from 1603 to 1868, it is estimated that there were around 1.5 million samurais.

However, as the end of the period approached, the number of samurais decreased due to the political and social changes that were taking place in Japan.

Additionally, within the samurai class, there were hierarchies based on wealth and power, and only the most powerful samurais could afford to have horses and fight on horseback.

17

In the Edo era (1603-1868), male homosexuality among samurais or between a samurai and his apprentice was common and not frowned upon in Japanese society at the time.

This practice was known as "wakashudo," which translates to "the way of the young."

The term refers to a romantic and sexual relationship between a young man (wakashu) and an older man (shudo), where the wakashu is the passive partner in the relationship.

This practice was considered part of the education and training of the young samurai, and it was believed to be important for establishing a strong bond between the master and the apprentice.

In fact, it was thought that the wakashu should be initiated into sex by an older and experienced man, who would guide him in his formation as a samurai and help him grow as a person.

However, it should also be noted that the practice of wakashudo was not without its criticisms or controversies in society at the time.

Some writings and literary works of the era addressed the topic in a critical or satirical manner, and some samurais considered the practice to be a form of weakness or lack of manliness.

18

The sword testing was a common practice among samurais to ensure their weapon was sharp and sturdy enough for use in combat.

This practice was known as "tameshigiri" and involved cutting objects such as tatami mats, bamboo, straw, and in some cases, human bodies.

However, the use of human corpses for sword testing was considered a very extreme act and was not a widespread practice in samurai society.

In fact, the samurai code of honor (bushido) stated that respect for human life was a fundamental value.

Although in times of war, some samurais might display more violent and less respectful behavior towards enemies, using the bodies of the deceased to test their swords was uncommon.

19

!A Poem Before Dying.

If a samurai fell into enemy hands, he would commit suicide.

The samurai would express his last words through a poem and then take his own life.

Others could assist him by beheading to hasten the process.

Poem:

Let my words be the echo, of my soul in its farewell, expressing what I feel, before my life comes to an end.

Let my poem be my witness, to what I loved and what I lost, reflecting my free spirit, before my soul slips away.

And if someone is to assist me, let them do so with compassion, let my death not be in vain, and may my legacy continue in my song.

Thus, like the samurai of old, who found his destiny in death, I too wish to leave my mark, in this world that was my path.

20

Traditional Japanese clothing is rich in detail and symbolism, and has evolved over the centuries.

The kimono, which literally means "thing to wear," is Japan's most iconic garment and is worn by both men and women.

The kimono is a long, loose tunic that is fastened with a belt called an obi.

It is made from various types of fabric, such as silk, cotton, linen, or rayon, and can be decorated with prints, embroidery, or dyes.

The hakama is a garment worn over the kimono and consists of a pair of wide, pleated trousers.

Originally used mainly for horseback riding, it has become a formal and ceremonial garment over time.

It is still used in martial arts and ceremonies such as weddings or graduations.

Wooden sandals, known as Geta, are a traditional type of footwear mainly worn in summer to protect the feet from ground moisture and keep them cool.

They have a raised wooden sole with two small platforms that insert between the big toe and the second toe, and are joined by a leather strap.

For more formal occasions, men also wear a jacket over the kimono and hakama known as Kamishimo.

This garment consists of a long jacket that fastens at the front with a series of buttons, and short, puffed trousers that tie around the waist with a cord.

The Kamishimo is mainly used in traditional ceremonies and festivals, and its design can vary depending on the region and historical period.

Regarding accessories, traditional Japanese clothing includes a variety of elements, such as the obi, zori (a type of thong sandal), haori (a type of short jacket), hanten (a type of padded jacket), nagajuban (a type of undershirt), juban (an undershirt for the kimono), among others.

Each of these elements has a specific meaning and function within the traditional Japanese outfit.

21

Samurai Children.

Children born into samurai families began their training from a very young age.

Gradually, they were instilled with the values of bushido and sent to study disciplines such as calligraphy, the tea ceremony, and meditation.

By the age of 7, they could wear hakamas but were not yet recognized as adults, so they could only practice with wooden sword replicas and nothing more.

When they reached the age of 15, they underwent a ceremony called "Genpuku" through which they were given their first swords, allowed to wear adult clothing, and also had their hair cut changed.

In this ceremony, they were also granted the right to marry and at the same time, they were given all the responsibilities of an adult.

22

The Last Samurai.

At the end of the 19th century, Japan underwent a profound cultural, economic, social, and political transformation, known as the Meiji era, which brought it in line with many aspects of the Western powers of the time.

One of the direct consequences of these transformations was the persecution and systematic elimination of the samurais, considering them destabilizing elements and obsolete remnants of past eras.

For this reason, Saigo Takamori, a prestigious samurai who had served in government roles during Emperor Matshuito's reforms, outraged and horrified by the persecutions of his comrades, decided to lead the so-called "Satsuma Rebellion" against the imperial army.

It was in the final battle of Shiroyama, on September 24, 1877, when Takamori, with his army completely decimated and himself gravely wounded by machine gun bullets, decided, for personal honor, to commit seppuku, going down in history as the true last samurai.

23

Although their origin is uncertain, it is known that the samurais emerged from a humble social class and that their role in Japanese society evolved over time.

In the beginning, aristocratic warriors who participated in wars were known as "Bushi."

On the other hand, "samurais" were originally servants from the lower social class who worked on the properties of feudal lords or daimyos.

These servants were responsible for the security and protection of the lords and their properties and often fought as warriors in battles.

Over time, clans began to structure themselves more formally, and wars between clans occurred.

It was then that loyalty to a lord or "daimyo" became a supreme principle for warriors, and the warriors fighting in the name of a daimyo began to be called samurais.

As the samurais gained more power and prestige, a unique culture developed around them.

Samurais followed a strict ethical and moral code known as "bushido," which emphasized loyalty, bravery, honesty, self-discipline, and honor.

A distinct aesthetic and lifestyle also developed, which included traditional clothing, martial arts, and poetry.

24

Oda Nobunaga was a prominent Japanese feudal lord who lived in the 16th century and is remembered as one of the main unifiers of Japan.

While it is true that he is considered a hero by many, it is also true that his legacy is controversial due to his authoritarian style of governance.

During his military career, Oda Nobunaga dedicated himself to expanding his territory and eliminating his rivals.

In the end, he managed to unify much of the country, ending a period of civil wars that had lasted for over a century.

This earned him the admiration of many Japanese, who saw him as a savior of Japan.

However, his method of unification was highly controversial.

To consolidate his power, Oda Nobunaga carried out a series of political and social reforms that ultimately solidified the class-based society.

One of these reforms was the prohibition of the use of the katana, the samurai sword, among the civilian population.

This meant that peasants and other people from lower social classes could no longer have access to it, making their social ascent more difficult.

Another control measure implemented by Oda Nobunaga was the registration of all citizens, to maintain more effective control over them.

Thus, he became an authoritarian leader who ruled with an iron fist, which has been compared to the governance style of a dictator.

In conclusion, Oda Nobunaga is a historical figure who has been viewed in different ways by the Japanese.

While it is true that he unified Japan and is considered by many a hero, it is also true that his authoritarian style of governance is the subject of controversy due to the reforms he carried out to solidify the class-based society and consolidate his power.

25

The origin of ninjas is a subject of debate, and there are several theories regarding it.

However, one of the most accepted theories is that ninjas emerged during the Sengoku period (1467-1603), a time of intense civil wars in Japan.

During this period, samurais began to resort to unconventional tactics to gain an advantage on the battlefield.

One of the factors that led to the emergence of ninjas was the increasing importance of military intelligence.

Samurai clans began to realize that they could not win a war solely with brute force but also needed information about the enemy and their movements.

Therefore, they began training men who could infiltrate enemy lines and gather information.

These men, who specialized in espionage and sabotage, were known as "shinobi," which means "people who act in the shadows."

Over time, this term evolved to "ninja."

In terms of their attire, ninjas were known for wearing comfortable and dark-colored clothing that allowed them to move stealthily.

They also used specialized tools and weapons such as shuriken (throwing stars), kusarigama (a weapon consisting of a sickle attached to a chain), and kunai (a throwing knife).

26

The Samurai of Seville.

In Spain, more specifically in Seville (Coria del Río), there is samurai descent.

The samurai responsible for this is named "Date Masamune," a first aristocratic warrior open to relations with foreigners and Christianity.

His goal was to collect advanced engineering knowledge from Spain and Portugal.

He participated in building the fleet "San Juan Bautista" with which he set out to explore the world.

Eventually, he settled in Seville to live.

His descendants were known by the surname "Japón" due to pronunciation difficulties.

27

Samurais vs. Spaniards.

The Battles of Cagayán were a series of military confrontations that took place in 1582 between the Spanish Armada of the Philippines under the command of Captain Juan Pablo de Carrión and pirates, including Chinese, Korean, Filipino, and Japanese, led, according to Spanish records, by a certain Tay Fusa.

The battles took place near the Cagayán River as a response to the pirate raids on the coasts of Luzon and ended in a Spanish victory.

This event was notable for pitting arquebusiers, pikemen, and sword-and-buckler men against a contingent made up of Japanese and Chinese pirates.

28

Battles of Cagayán: The First Clash.

As they passed by the cape of the island, the Spanish fleet spotted a large Japanese junk that had just ravaged the coast and plundered the inhabitants.

The flagship galley then advanced to intercept it, despite the Japanese ship being larger and carrying more fighters.

After catching up with the junk, the Capitana fired a barrage of artillery, causing the first deaths and injuries, and then grappled onto the Japanese ship to initiate a boarding assault, personally led by Carrión himself.

However, the pirates, superior in number and armed not only with melee weapons but also with their own arquebuses provided by the Portuguese, managed to halt the Spanish advance and repel the assault.

The situation turned for the worse for the Armada to the extent that the Spanish had to retreat, and the pirates conducted their own boarding of the galley's deck.

To regain the initiative, Carrión's soldiers established a defensive position at the stern, forming a barrier with pikemen in front and arquebusiers and musketeers behind.

Carrión then cut the halyard of the main sail, which fell across the deck, creating an additional trench to take cover behind.

Their formation and mastery of firearms, along with the robustness of their armors compared to their adversaries, aided them.

This position eventually allowed them to regroup and regain ground through volleys of gunfire and hand-to-hand charges, pushing the pirates back towards the junk.

Coinciding with this counterattack, the San Yusepe arrived, firing at the Japanese ship and eliminating the shooters still harassing the Capitana.

Realizing the battle was lost, the pirates abandoned their ships and jumped into the water to try to swim to shore, resulting in many drowning due to their armors, which, although lighter, were cumbersome for swimming.

The Spanish also suffered their first casualties, including the captain of the galley, Pedro Lucas.

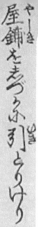

29

Battles of Cagayán: Battle at the Tajo.

Having regrouped, the Spanish flotilla continued along the Tajo River (the name of the Grande de Cagayán River) and encountered Tay Fusa's fleet of 18 junks, which had also built fortifications at the river's mouth, totaling between 600 and 1000 men.

Carrión managed to lure them upstream, away from their advantageous positions, and there the two contingents fought at a distance for hours until the more powerful and better-handled Western cannons allowed their owners to prevail.

It is estimated that about 200 Japanese were killed or wounded in the exchange.

The Spaniards disembarked at a bend in the river to take positions near the bulk of the enemy forces, building a trench and placing the galley's cannons in it, continuing to fire.

Seeing themselves strategically outmatched, the wokou pirates decided to negotiate surrender, but Carrión refused and ordered them to leave Luzón.

The pirates then responded by asking for a gold indemnity for the losses they would suffer if they left, to which Carrión gave another firm refusal.

With negotiations broken, the Japanese decided to attack the Spanish land positions with several hundred soldiers, relying on their huge numerical superiority over the defenders (400-800 pirates against 40 soldiers and 20 sailors).

However, the trench withstood the first two assaults.

The Japanese resorted to the tactic of grasping the shafts of the pikes to make their way or take them, so the Spanish pikemen and halberdiers opted to smear grease on the wood during the pause between skirmishes, making them slippery and harder to grab.

These assaults were followed by a third, more desperate one, with both sides' gunpowder reserves exhausted, where hand-to-hand combat took place at the fortifications, but the result was again a Spanish victory.

Although the Spaniards had already lost at least 10 soldiers, the Japanese casualties by this point were much higher, leading them to desist from the attack and commence their final retreat.

30

Siege of Moji.

This was an attempt to capture the castle in this region during the Mori clan's campaigns in 1561.

Due to a brief participation by the Portuguese on one side, it has been considered the first hostile contact between Europeans and Japanese.

The castle was originally built by Ōuchi Yoshinaga, who committed suicide in 1557 with the advance of the Mori forces.

The fortification was captured by Mōri Motonari in 1557, but his position there was unstable: Ōtomo Yoshishige recaptured the castle in September 1559, only to fall back into Mori hands through the actions of Kobayakawa Takakage and Ura Munekatsu shortly after.

To bring the castle back under the Otomo clan's control, Ōtomo Sōrin carried out a siege in alliance with a flotilla of Portuguese traders, who provided three ships of 500 tons and 300 men each.

Hostilities began with a series of bombardments from the Portuguese ships, allowing the Otomo contingent to surround the castle unopposed.

The siege continued with prolonged cannon fire, but it was interrupted when the Portuguese ran out of ammunition, at which point they lifted anchor and left the battle.

Deprived of their tactical advantage, the Otomo clan was attacked by enemy reinforcements, who managed to break the siege with a joint action and strengthen the castle's position.

On October 10, Sorin made a desperate assault on the castle walls, but they were repelled and were forced to definitively abandon the siege.

31

Battle of Fukuda Bay.

In 1565, a flotilla of samurais from the Matsura clan attempted to capture 2 Portuguese ships in Fukuda but was repelled and defeated.

Due to the lack of preparation of the Portuguese ships, the Japanese were able to approach and board them without difficulty.

One of the first samurais to climb aboard, identifying Pereira as the captain, fired a musket shot that hit the Portuguese in the head, who only survived because his helmet withstood the impact.

The crew took the captain to his cabin while trying to repel the boarding.

The courage and numerical superiority of the attackers momentarily overwhelmed them, to the point that a group of Japanese accessed the cabin, took Pereira hostage, and tried to take his desk, probably in search of his commercial documents.

Only then did the Portuguese begin to recover, managing to rescue the captain and kill the Japanese attackers.

At that moment, taking advantage of the Japanese fleet concentrating on attacking the carrack closest to their positions, the Portuguese galleon maneuvered to flank them and unleashed its artillery against the Matsura contingent.

The large number of Japanese forces, as well as the flimsy construction of their ships, made them very vulnerable targets to the powerful European cannons, so the counterattack caused them enormous damage, particularly as they were caught between two fires.

Two hours of cannon fire later, and after losing 3 complete sekibuns, more than 70 men, and about 200 wounded, the Japanese broke ranks and retreated.

32

In samurai culture, a person's full name could be quite extensive and complex, and usually reflected their social position, titles and honors, as well as the region or clan to which they belonged.

Typically, a samurai's full name consisted of several parts, which included:

-The family name: usually indicated affiliation with a clan or family.

-The personal name: used to distinguish each individual within the clan or family.

-The courtesy name: a nickname or alias used to refer to someone more familiarly.

-The title: indicated the person's social or military position, such as "daimyo" (feudal lord), "shogun" (military commander), "hatamoto" (high-ranking samurai), among others.

-The name of the province or territory: used to identify the region of origin of the samurai.

-The name of the land or castle: indicated the fief or domain that the samurai owned or served.

For example, the full name of Oda Nobunaga, one of the most powerful feudal lords of the Sengoku era, was Oda Kazusanosuke Saburo Nobunaga.

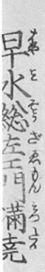

33

The "Hagakure" is a book that compiles a series of thoughts, reflections, and teachings of Yamamoto Tsunemoto, who lived in Japan during the Edo period (1603-1868), a time when samurais had a significant influence on Japanese society.

The book was written in the 18th century but wasn't published until many years later, when it was discovered by a Buddhist priest named Tsuramoto Tashiro.

Although it was not very popular in its time, the "Hagakure" has become a classic text of samurai philosophy and has been highly influential in Japanese culture.

The book addresses themes such as courage, loyalty, honor, death, and duty, and emphasizes the importance of discipline, self-control, and perseverance in a samurai's life.

The "Hagakure" is also known for its ideas about bushido, the ethical and moral code of the samurais.

It describes how a samurai should live and act in different situations, such as in war, at court, or in everyday life, and how he should maintain his honor and loyalty to his lord.

Although it has become a highly respected and quoted book in popular culture, some people have criticized the "Hagakure" for its focus on death and self-destruction, and for promoting values such as violence and blind obedience.

34

The process of making Japanese steel is very complex and is carried out using an ancestral technique known as "tatara."

In this process, three different types of iron ore are used, which are melted together in a clay furnace in a controlled environment.

The precise combination of these minerals and the blacksmith's skill in controlling the temperature and cooking time are key to achieving high-quality Tamahagane steel.

This steel has a high carbon content, which gives it hardness and strength while allowing it to remain flexible.

Additionally, its unique molecular structure allows the sword blade to have a high edge retention capacity, meaning that the blade maintains its sharpness for a long time.

Japanese steel is also used in other fields, such as the manufacturing of high-quality tools and kitchen utensils.

The production process of Japanese steel is highly valued and is considered an art form in itself.

35

Takeda Shingen (1521-1573) was a warrior and samurai leader who ruled the Takeda clan in the province of Kai, in central Japan, during the Sengoku period.

He was one of the greatest and most powerful daimyos (feudal lords) of Japan, and he is considered one of the best military strategists of the time.

Shingen was a respected and admired leader for his military skills, earning a reputation as a cold and calculating man on the battlefield.

He was famous for his innovative tactics, including the use of mobile units and deception, and for his ability to quickly adapt to the changing conditions of war.

One of Shingen's greatest achievements was the conquest of Suwa Castle in 1542, which allowed him to extend his influence in the Shinano region.

He also defeated other rival feudal lords, including Uesugi Kenshin, with whom he maintained a long and famous rivalry.

Shingen died in 1573 at the age of 52 due to an illness, leading to the decline of the Takeda clan and their subsequent defeat at the Battle of Nagashino in 1575.

Despite his premature death, his legacy as one of the greatest samurai leaders in Japanese history continues to be remembered and celebrated today.

36

In the West, an idealized version of the samurai code, or "Bushido," has become popularized.

This romantic image of the noble, loyal, and honorable warrior has been conveyed through literature, film, and video games, but it's important to remember that the samurai code was much more complex and varied than depicted in these representations.

Each clan and each samurai had their own interpretation of Bushido, which could differ in some aspects.

For example, some samurais considered loyalty to their lord as the most important, while others valued honesty and integrity more.

The idea of accepting death as one's ultimate fate was common to all, but there were also differences in understanding this concept.

Moreover, it's important to note that Bushido was not a set of rigid rules, but rather a set of ethical principles that were to be interpreted and applied by each samurai in their daily life.

In this sense, the idealized image of the samurai as a noble and honorable warrior might not always have been the reality.

As in any society, there were also corrupt, dishonest, or cruel samurais who did not follow the ethical principles of Bushido.

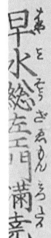

37

The kabuto or samurai helmet was a fundamental piece of the samurai warrior's armor.

It was designed to protect the head and neck on the battlefield.

Kabutos were constructed from various materials such as leather, iron, bronze, or gold, depending on the rank and wealth of the samurai.

Designs also varied based on the historical period and the region of Japan.

The kabuto had a characteristic shape, with a crest on the top that represented the samurai's position on the battlefield and was often decorated with adornments and symbolic elements representing the clan, family, or deity worshiped.

Additionally, it had a facial mask called mempo, which could have different shapes and designs and served to intimidate the enemy and protect the warrior's face.

The process of making a kabuto was very laborious and required the skill of specialized artisans.

Some kabutos were so elaborate that they could take months or even years to complete.

Today, the kabuto remains a symbol of Japanese culture and is used in ceremonies and festivals to showcase the heritage and tradition of the samurai.

38

The collection of heads, also known as "tsurushi-kubi" in Japanese, was a ritual practiced by some samurais on the battlefield.

It involved decapitating defeated enemies and collecting their heads as a way to demonstrate bravery and skill in war.

After the battle, the heads were taken to the castle of their lord to be presented as a war trophy.

It is said that this ritual began during the "sengoku jidai" (Warring States period) and continued through the 17th and 18th centuries.

Although not all samurais practiced it, it was common in some clans and regions of Japan.

On some occasions, samurais not only collected the heads of their enemies but also displayed them publicly as a way to intimidate their enemies and gain respect and prestige in their community.

This practice also had a spiritual dimension, as it was believed that by cutting off an enemy's head, their soul was released, and one could obtain power and protection from the gods.

39

Paying homage to the adversary, known in Japanese as "gyaku-gire," was a common practice in samurai culture.

It was an act of respect and recognition towards a defeated enemy, typically carried out in cases of duels to the death or battles where both combatants knew the outcome would be lethal.

After achieving victory, the victorious samurai would usually bow before the body of the defeated opponent and light incense in their helmet as a sign of respect and tribute to their bravery and skill in combat.

Then, they would proceed to conduct a quick funeral, placing the adversary's body in a resting position and covering it with a white cloth.

This ritual was a demonstration of the importance that samurai culture placed on skill in combat and personal honor.

The fact that the victor paid homage to their defeated adversary showed that victory was not just a matter of skill or strength but also of respect and consideration for the opponent.

40

Samurai Armor Resistance.

The breastplates of samurai armor were capable of withstanding the impact of approximately two arquebus shots.

The complete samurai armor weighed between 15 and 25 kg.

It's important to note that the resistance of samurai armor depended on the material used in its manufacture and the quality of the work done by the armorer.

Originally, samurai armors were made of iron plates, which offered good protection against sword cuts and other melee weapon attacks.

However, with the advent of firearms, samurais began experimenting with more resistant materials like steel and adding metal plates in the most vulnerable areas.

Despite their resistance, samurai armors were not invincible and could be penetrated by more powerful firearms or by well-aimed blows with blunt weapons.

Additionally, the weight of the armor could be a disadvantage in prolonged combat situations, especially in warm climates.

41

Mitsubishi had its roots in a samurai family.

During the Edo period in Japan, the Iwasaki family, originating from the Tosa clan, was engaged in shipbuilding and maritime trade.

With the onset of the Meiji era, the Iwasaki family quickly adapted to changes in the economy and technology, and in 1870, they founded the Mitsubishi company, which initially focused on shipbuilding and engineering.

The company rapidly expanded and diversified into a wide range of industries, including automobile manufacturing, heavy machinery, electronics, and chemicals.

Today, Mitsubishi is one of the largest and most successful companies in Japan and has a global presence in a variety of industries.

42

Before the 16th century, samurais used the bow and arrow as their primary weapon, as it was considered a more effective and lethal tool than the sword.

Additionally, the use of the spear was also very common, as it allowed warriors to maintain a safe distance from their opponents and attack from afar.

However, with the arrival of the Portuguese in Japan and the introduction of firearms, samurais began to use them increasingly in battle.

Although initially considered as support weapons and not replacing the sword, over time they became the primary weapon, especially among poorer samurais who could not afford high-quality swords.

Even so, the katana remained an important and symbolic weapon for samurais, used in duels and as a status symbol.

Moreover, samurais were also trained in the use of other weapons like the wakizashi, a shorter sword, and the tanto, a short-bladed dagger used in close combat.

43

Samurais preferred riding horses of the Kiso Uma breed, originating from the Kiso region in Japan.

These horses were small and sturdy, standing at about 1.2 meters tall and weighing an average of 400 kg.

Despite their size, they were very resilient and capable of enduring long hours of battle and travel.

The reason why samurais preferred Kiso Uma was due to their maneuverability in tight spaces, as most battles in Japan were fought in mountainous and wooded terrains.

Moreover, they were easier to feed and maintain than the larger and more elegant horses used in Europe and other parts of the world.

Despite their unimposing appearance, Kiso Uma were highly valued by samurais and considered a symbol of loyalty and bravery.

Even today, in some parts of Japan, races and competitions are organized with Kiso Uma horses as a way to keep their tradition and legacy alive.

44

Samurais received remuneration in the form of rice, measured in koku.

One koku represented the amount of rice needed to feed a person for one year, estimated at around 150 kilograms of rice.

Koku was also a unit of measurement for tax and rice production.

The system of remuneration in koku for samurais was part of a system of honor and hierarchy within feudal Japanese society.

The more humble samurais received a few dozen kokus per year, while the more powerful and higher-ranking samurais could receive many thousands of kokus.

The level of power and status of a samurai was reflected in the amount of kokus they received.

In addition to receiving rice as remuneration, samurais could also receive land, titles, and other forms of reward for their services to their feudal lords.

Although samurais were a privileged class in feudal Japanese society, they were also subject to a strict code of conduct known as bushido, which emphasized loyalty, honor, and bravery.

45

Samurais walked on the left side of the streets in Japan during the feudal period, and this custom originated for practical reasons related to carrying their weapons.

Samurais wore their swords on their left hip, and by walking on the left side of the street, they could avoid their weapons clashing with the weapons of other samurais who also carried their swords on the left.

Additionally, walking on the left side also allowed them to have their right hand free to quickly draw their weapon in case of a confrontation.

Although the custom of walking on the left side of the streets is no longer relevant for most people in modern Japan, it is believed that this practice influenced the Japanese government's decision to adopt left-hand driving in the 1920s.

It is said that the measure was taken to accommodate imported vehicles that were driven on the left, and also to ensure that drivers had a better view of the road and could protect themselves from samurai sword attacks.

Today, Japan is one of the few countries in the world that still has left-hand driving.

46

Samurai fashion and style of dress had a significant impact on Japanese fashion during the feudal era.

Samurais were known for their fighting skills, and their manner of dressing was adapted to their needs for freedom of movement and speed to defend themselves in case of a surprise attack.

The traditional attire of a samurai consisted of a silk or linen kimono, wide trousers called hakama, and wooden sandals known as geta or zori.

The hakama was a wide and loose garment worn over the kimono, allowing for extensive freedom of movement in the legs.

The wooden sandals provided a solid and elevated sole that enabled samurais to walk easily over uneven or muddy surfaces.

The color and design of the kimono and hakama were also important in samurai fashion.

Dark colors, like black and dark blue, were popular as they were more practical and less conspicuous.

However, some samurais also preferred bright colors and striking patterns as a way to show their status and wealth.

In addition to their clothing, samurais also wore accessories like helmets and facial masks for protection in battle.

These accessories were also important for showing a samurai's rank and position in feudal society.

Today, some elements of samurai dressing style remain popular in modern Japanese fashion.

Hakama and wooden sandals are still used in ceremonies and popular festivals.

47

Regarding their physique, the samurais of the 16th century were not especially powerful.

Unlike the European warriors of the time, who tended to be tall and muscular, samurais were generally shorter and slimmer.

The average height of a samurai of the time was around 160 centimeters, although some could reach 165 centimeters.

Slimness was sought in a samurai because agility was considered more important than brute strength in combat.

Samurais trained in martial arts like kenjutsu (swordsmanship with a katana), kyujutsu (archery), jujutsu (hand-to-hand combat), and naginatajutsu (use of the naginata, a long spear with a curved blade at the end).

In addition to physical training, samurais also practiced meditation and mental discipline to develop concentration and self-control.

In general, the life of a samurai was centered around preparation for combat and defending the honor and loyalty to their feudal lord.

48

Chiburi is a movement used in Japanese martial arts, particularly in the handling of the katana (the Japanese sword).

It is a ritual movement performed after a confrontation or combat with the purpose of shaking off the blood from the sword's blade.

The word Chiburi is composed of two parts: "chi" (血), meaning blood, and "buri" (振り), meaning to shake or flick.

Therefore, Chiburi specifically refers to the technique of shaking the blood off the sword's blade.

In the context of samurai, Chiburi was considered an important movement to demonstrate respect towards the defeated opponent and towards the sword itself.

Samurai believed that the enemy's blood on the sword blade could damage the steel, so it was important to shake it off before sheathing the katana.

Today, Chiburi is used in many Japanese martial arts as part of sword-handling technique.

In Iaido, a discipline focused on the technique of unsheathing and cutting with the katana, Chiburi is an important part of the movement sequence.

Kendo, a sport based on the use of bamboo swords to simulate combat, also uses Chiburi as part of its technique.

Even in martial arts that do not involve swords, like Aikido, Chiburi can be used as a way to demonstrate respect and discipline.

49

Although Chiburi was effective in removing most of the dirt from the katana blade, a small amount of residue often remained on the surface of the blade.

To effectively clean the katana, samurai used kaishi [懐紙], a special type of paper that was always carried inside the kimono.

Kaishi were handkerchief-sized sheets of paper made from rice paper or hemp paper, used for cleaning the katana blade.

Samurai usually had several kaishi folded into a small packet and kept inside their kimono, close to their heart, to keep them dry and protected.

Kaishi also had other uses, such as for writing notes, as napkins for meals, or as handkerchiefs for wiping sweat.

Furthermore, they were considered an essential element of a samurai's equipment, and it was seen as disrespectful for a samurai not to carry kaishi with them at all times.

50

The Bokken is a type of Japanese sword used as a replica of the Katana, but instead of being made of metal, it is made of wood.

This wooden sword is very popular in Japanese martial arts, especially in Kendo and Aikido.

The history of the Bokken dates back to the Japanese feudal era, when samurai used it as a training tool to practice their sword skills without the risk of severe injuries.

During that time, metal swords were very expensive and difficult to obtain, so the Bokken was a more economical and safer alternative for training.

The Bokken is made in different sizes and materials, but hardwoods like oak, beech, or ash are generally used for its construction.

It is designed to have a weight and balance similar to a real sword, allowing practitioners to effectively develop their technique and sword-handling skills.

The use of the Bokken is an integral part of the practice of Kendo and Aikido. In Kendo, the Bokken is used to practice sword techniques and to develop posture and body movement.

In Aikido, the Bokken is used to practice cutting movements and defensive techniques against an armed opponent.

In addition to being a training tool for Japanese martial arts, the Bokken is also used in some forms of meditation and spiritual practices like Kyudo (Japanese archery) and Iaido (the art of katana unsheathing).

51

In feudal Japan, Kago 【駕籠】 were a type of palanquin used for transporting people, especially by members of the nobility and samurai.

Kago consisted of a covered and enclosed structure made of bamboo or wood, carried by two or more men who held the palanquin on their shoulders or on a pole on their backs.

Kago were a very popular form of transportation during the Tokugawa era, which lasted from the 17th to the 19th century.

During this period, samurai and nobles used Kago for traveling around the city and countryside, as well as for attending social events and important ceremonies.

Kago were symbols of status and wealth, and people of high society often competed to have the most elegant and decorated palanquins.

The Kago of the samurai, for example, were often adorned with the family crest and other status symbols and were often painted with bright colors and intricate designs.

In addition to transporting people, Kago were also used to carry objects and goods.

Cargo Kago, which were larger and more robust, were used to transport supplies and products between cities and towns.

Today, Kago are no longer used as a means of transportation in Japan.

However, palanquins can still be found in use in some rural areas and in traditional festivals and celebrations.

Additionally, Kago have become a popular tourist attraction in Japan, with some places offering palanquin rides for visitors to experience the tradition and history of this form of transportation.

52

Zen Buddhism, also known as Chan Buddhism in China, is a branch of Mahayana Buddhism that originated in China and later spread to other countries such as Japan, Korea, and Vietnam.

The philosophy of Zen Buddhism emphasizes meditation and the direct practice of enlightenment, rather than scholarship or reading of sacred texts.

In Japan, Zen Buddhism arrived around the 12th century and became an important part of Samurai culture.

Zen meditation became a popular practice among the samurai, as it allowed them to cultivate the concentration and mental tranquility necessary for battle.

Zen also emphasized the importance of living in the present moment, a valuable skill for samurai who needed to be always alert and ready to act.

In addition to meditation, Zen Buddhism also taught the importance of self-discipline and self-control.

Samurai, who often faced death on the battlefield, found in Zen philosophy a way to accept death and overcome the fear of dying.

Zen also emphasized the importance of compassion and empathy, values that the samurai considered crucial to their code of honor and their service to others.

Overall, Zen Buddhism had a significant impact on the philosophy and culture of the samurai.

Meditation and the practice of self-discipline and self-control became important parts of samurai training, and many samurai found in Zen a way to enrich their spiritual life and find meaning and purpose in their service.

53

During the 13th century, the Mongol Empire, under the leadership of Kublai Khan, attempted to invade Japan on two occasions, in 1274 and 1281.

These invasions were known as the Mongol Invasions of Japan. In both cases, the samurai, along with other warriors and the aid of typhoons, managed to repel the invasion attempts.

In the first invasion, the Mongols arrived on the island of Kyushu with a force of approximately 40,000 men and managed to establish a beachhead.

However, the samurai and other Japanese warriors, led by the Kamakura shogunate, fought valiantly to expel the invaders.

Finally, a typhoon struck the coast and destroyed much of the Mongol fleet, allowing the Japanese to win the battle.

In the second invasion, the Mongols returned with a much larger force of approximately 140,000 men.

The samurai and other Japanese warriors once again fought with great bravery and skill, but the Mongols managed to establish a beachhead on the island of Kyushu.

However, a typhoon, known as the kamikaze ('divine wind'), hit the coast and destroyed much of the Mongol fleet, enabling the Japanese to win the battle again.

Despite these military triumphs, internal strife and conflicts among samurai clans continued in Japan during this period.

These conflicts, known as the Japanese Civil Wars, lasted from the 14th to the 16th century and led to significant political and social instability in the country.

Despite these challenges, the samurai continued to play an important role in Japan's history, and their legacy remains an integral part of Japanese culture and identity to this day.

54

**From the late 16th century in Japan, samurai were the
only ones entitled to carry a sword.**

The Sword Hunt, an initiative promoted by the emperor's regent,
Toyotomi Hideyoshi, in 1588, aimed to prohibit the non-samurai
population from using weapons, especially swords, thereby controlling
any potential peasant rebellions.

The Sword Hunt was a massive campaign of weapon confiscation
across Japan.

Hideyoshi ordered peasants to surrender their weapons and swords,
under the penalty of death for non-compliance.

The confiscated weapons were melted down and converted into
monuments and buildings, and only samurai were allowed to retain
their swords.

Additionally, samurai had to show their swords to the guards at the
local castle to prove legal possession.

Through this measure, Hideyoshi sought to strengthen government
control over the population and ensure the samurai's monopoly on the
use of force.

Thereafter, carrying a sword became an exclusive symbol of the
samurai, enhancing their sense of power and status in Japanese
society.

The Sword Hunt became a significant milestone in Japan's history,
laying the groundwork for the future consolidation of samurai power
in the country.

Moreover, the prohibition of weapon use by peasants contributed to
social peace, though it also increased social inequality and oppression
of the people.

55

Samurai were known for their toughness on the battlefield, but it's important to note that there were certain norms and codes of conduct that governed their behavior in war.

One of the most important principles was bushido, an ethical code that established values such as loyalty, honor, honesty, and respect.

According to this code, death in combat was preferable to defeat or dishonor.

However, it is true that during the 16th-century Korean campaigns, some samurai engaged in very cruel practices, such as beheading enemies and preserving their noses as trophies.

These actions were seen as a way to demonstrate bravery and courage on the battlefield, but also as a means to instill fear in enemies.

It's important to recognize that these practices were considered barbaric even by the standards of the time, and not all samurai engaged in them.

In fact, some samurai leaders, like Oda Nobunaga, tried to prohibit these practices and promote more humane behavior on the battlefield.

56

There are several katanas that have been sold at auctions for very high prices.

Here are some of the most notable ones along with their prices and features:

–**"The Jewel of Heaven,"**: a 17th-century Japanese katana, was sold at an auction in Hong Kong in 2015 for a record price of $16.9 million. The sword is made of carbon steel and measures 1.3 meters in length.

–**"The Sword of Goro Nyudo Masamune,"**: a 14th-century Japanese katana, was sold at an auction in New York in 1992 for $418,000. The sword was crafted by the legendary swordsmith Masamune and has a length of 66.5 cm.

–**"The Dragon Sword,"**: a 17th-century Japanese katana, was sold at an auction at Christie's in 2016 for $602,500. The sword features a 76.5 cm long blade with engravings in gold and silver.

It's important to highlight that these katanas are considered works of art and historical relics, making them extremely valuable and highly sought after by collectors around the world.

57

There are several katana smiths in Japan who are highly recognized for their skill and mastery in the art of swordsmithing.

One of the most famous is Yoshindo Yoshihara, who belongs to a family of katana smiths dating back over 400 years.

Yoshihara has been named a Living National Treasure of Japan for his skill in forging katanas and his ability to preserve traditional techniques.

Another renowned smith is Sadatoshi Matsubara, known for his ability to create exceptionally strong and durable katanas.

Matsubara has won several awards for his work and is considered one of the best katana smiths today.

There are also other highly recognized katana smiths in Japan, such as Shoji Nishio, Yoshikazu Yoshioka, among others.

Overall, the art of katana forging is highly valued in Japan, and there are many talented smiths who have followed traditional techniques to create these iconic swords.

58

The cursed katana commonly referred to is known as the "Muramasa."

It is said that the sword possesses demonic powers and becomes bloodthirsty once its power is unleashed.

Legend has it that Muramasa swords were cursed by the blacksmith Muramasa himself, who was supposedly mad and filled with hate and rage.

Muramasa swords were so sharp that they were said to cut through the wind and leaves of trees, bestowing them with a kind of curse.

However, it's important to note that the idea of Muramasa swords being cursed is largely a creation of popular culture and fiction.

Historically, the Muramasa sword is considered a work of art and one of the sharpest and best-forged katanas in Japanese history.

Oscar Ratti and Adele Westbrook said that Muramasa "was a very skilled blacksmith, but with a violent and unbalanced mind bordering on madness, which has passed such imbalance to his blades."

59

Samurai smoked kiseru, which were small Japanese pipes made of metal or bamboo.

However, not all samurai smoked, and some considered the smoking habit unpleasant or inappropriate for their social status.

Regarding the substances smoked, tobacco was introduced to Japan in the 16th century and quickly became a popular choice among samurai.

Opium was also imported in the 17th century and became a popular substance among the common people, but not as much among the nobility.

On the other hand, cannabis was also grown in Japan, but its use was not as common as tobacco.

In general, it is believed that samurai smoked to relax and relieve stress after a battle or strenuous training, or simply to enjoy the flavor and aroma of different herbs.

60

Tennōheika Banzai! is an expression commonly associated with samurai, although in reality, it is a phrase that became popular during Japan's Showa era in the 20th century and was used as a war cry by the Japanese Imperial Army during World War II.

The phrase means "Long live the Emperor!" and was used to express loyalty and devotion to the Emperor, considered a divine figure by the Japanese.

However, samurai did not always shout this particular phrase.

In battle, it is believed that samurai shouted various slogans or war cries to motivate themselves and their comrades, as well as to intimidate their enemies.

These shouts could vary depending on the samurai clan they belonged to, the era they lived in, the geographical region, or even the individual.

In any case, the war cry was considered an important part of battle strategy, as it helped maintain morale and courage in moments of extreme tension and danger.

61

Kombucha is a fermented and carbonated beverage made from sweetened tea and a symbiotic culture of bacteria and yeast (SCOBY).

Although kombucha is believed to have originated in Central Asia, its consumption has spread worldwide today.

Regarding the samurai, some historical records suggest that they drank kombucha before battle to gain an energy boost.

Additionally, kombucha was also considered beneficial for health and was used to treat a variety of ailments.

It's noteworthy that kombucha contained a small amount of alcohol due to the fermentation process, but it was generally considered a non-alcoholic beverage.

Today, kombucha has become very popular as a healthy and refreshing drink.

62

In samurai culture, long hair was considered a symbol of honor and social status.

Samurai warriors wore their hair long as part of their code of conduct and identity.

Long hair was also practical for samurai, as they could tie it in a knot to keep their helmet in place during battles.

The traditional hairstyle for samurai was the "chonmage," which involved shaving the head on the sides and leaving a portion of hair on top, which was combed and tied into a topknot.

This hairstyle became a status symbol in Japanese society, and only samurai and some government workers were allowed to wear it.

However, with the abolition of the feudal system and the fall of the samurai in the 19th century, the traditional samurai hairstyle was banned.

From then on, Western fashion became more popular, and hair was cut in shorter styles.

63

Cutting one's hair was seen as an act of humility and renunciation of social status, and it was considered a symbol of defeat and loss of honor.

In some cases, samurai cut their hair as a way to show penance or remorse for a dishonorable action or for failing to adhere to the bushido code of conduct.

They could also cut their hair before a battle as a way of mentally preparing themselves and demonstrating their commitment to victory.

64

The traditional form of greeting among Japanese samurai was the bow, or respectful inclination, called "ojigi."

This gesture was a sign of respect and an indication of having no hostile intentions.

Ojigi was performed by bending the body forward from the waist, keeping the back straight, and the hands together and downward in front of the body.

The depth of the bow varied depending on the rank and relationship between the samurai greeting each other, but generally, it was deeper for superiors and shorter for inferiors.

In addition, samurai also commonly used the phrase "ojamashimasu" as a courtesy expression when entering someone's house or personal space.

This phrase roughly means "I apologize for intruding" and is used to show respect and avoid causing discomfort.

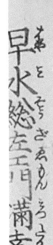

65

The traditional footwear of the samurai is known as tsuranuki, also called jikatabi.

These are high boots that cover the feet and ankles and have a separate compartment for the big toe, allowing for greater grip and stability while walking.

Although it is mentioned that tsuranuki could be made of bear skin, there were also variants made of fabric or canvas.

Samurai often wore these boots in combination with hakama, a wide and pleated pair of trousers, as well as with the traditional Japanese armor known as yoroi.

Besides their practical utility for war and fighting, tsuranuki was also a symbol of status and considered an integral part of the samurai attire.

Even today in Japan, modern versions of tsuranuki can be found, used for martial arts practice and as casual footwear.

66

**Samurai had a strong connection with nature,
and animals were very important in their culture and daily life.**

While there isn't a single animal that was essential for samurai, several creatures held prominent places in their symbolism and imagery.

One of the most representative animals for samurai is the dragon (Ryū).

In Japanese culture, the dragon symbolizes wisdom, protection, and power, and is considered an emblem of heroes and leaders alike.

Samurai often included depictions of dragons in their armor and other elements of their attire and weaponry.

Dragons were also associated with the Emperor of Japan, who was believed to descend from a lineage of divine dragons.

Another important animal for the samurai was the horse.

Samurai were expert riders, excelling in horsemanship and mounted battle.

Horses were essential for samurai, as they allowed rapid movement across the battlefield and enabled them to charge against their enemies with strength and determination.

Moreover, samurai greatly valued loyalty and fidelity, and the horse was a symbol of these qualities.

It's also said that samurai appreciated falcons and other birds of prey for their speed and precision in hunting, as well as their agility and elegance in flight.

Some samurai even bred and trained these birds for hunting and skill exhibitions.

67

Samurai were a privileged class of warriors in feudal Japanese society.

Their elevated status granted them certain privileges and rights not available to most of the population.

As you mention, the samurai's maxim was to serve their lord in the best way possible, giving them a sense of purpose and loyalty to their cause.

In addition to this, they had the right to carry two swords, known as daishō, which were a symbol of their warrior status and skill in combat.

The long sword (katana) was the primary one, and the short sword (wakizashi) was the secondary.

They were also allowed to bear a family name and were considered a noble caste.

Indeed, some samurai had noble ancestors and considered themselves of aristocratic lineage.

This gave them certain influence in society and made them more desirable as husbands for daughters of noble families.

Regarding the privilege of "permitted cut," it was a concession that allowed samurai to take justice into their own hands in certain situations.

If a samurai encountered someone breaking the law or committing a crime, they were permitted to kill that person without being punished by the law.

However, this concession was used sparingly, and samurai were expected to use it judiciously.

In addition to this, samurai had other rights and privileges, such as the right to ride horses and to use bows and arrows, giving them a tactical advantage in battle.

They also had certain tax benefits and were exempt from certain taxes.

68

In samurai culture, an apology was a very important and formal act, carried out in a specific and ceremonial manner.

The main purpose of the apology was to demonstrate remorse and humility to the offended person, and the offender was expected to take full responsibility for their mistake.

The most common method of apology in samurai culture was known as "dogeza," which involved kneeling on the ground and making a deep bow with the head low and hands placed on the ground.

This was a position of submission and humility, showing the offender's willingness to accept any punishment imposed and their desire to repair the harm caused.

In some cases, samurai might also offer a written apology, known as "shazan," in which they expressed their remorse and explained the cause of their mistake.

This written apology was considered very formal and was expected to be delivered personally to the recipient.

Overall, an apology in samurai culture was a serious matter and was expected to be offered sincerely and completely.

The goal was not only to repair the damage caused but also to restore harmony and dignity to both parties.

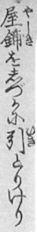

69

The shogun was the military leader of the samurai and held almost absolute power over feudal Japanese society.

The title of shogun originated in the 12th century, during the Heian period, when the general Minamoto no Yoritomo became the first shogun of Japan.

From then on, the shoguns ruled Japan for nearly 700 years.

The shogun was the supreme leader of the military forces and had the authority to make decisions on behalf of the emperor, who was theoretically the official ruler of Japan.

The power of the shogun was based on the support of the samurai, who were the most important and powerful warriors in feudal Japanese society.

In addition to leading the samurai in war, the shogun was also responsible for maintaining peace and stability in the country.

To achieve this, they established a centralized system of government and a legal code known as the "bushido code" that established the rules of conduct for the samurai.

The last shogun of Japan was Tokugawa Yoshinobu, who ruled until 1867 when Emperor Meiji regained power and began the Meiji era of Japanese history.

Although the title of shogun no longer exists in Japan, its legacy remains significant in Japanese culture and history.

70

**The Boshin War was an armed conflict fought
in Japan between 1868 and 1869.**

This war was a pivotal event in Japanese history, marking
the end of the Tokugawa Shogunate and the beginning of
the Meiji Era, a period of modernization and opening of
Japan to the world.

The conflict erupted after supporters of the Tokugawa
Shogunate tried to prevent the restoration of imperial
power.

The samurai of the imperial faction, who had remained in
the shadows for centuries, took up arms and fought
against the Shogunate's forces.

The war was fought throughout the country, from the
island of Hokkaido in the north to the island of Kyushu in
the south.

The imperial army, led by the young Emperor Meiji,
ultimately prevailed in the war.

After the victory, the Tokugawa Shogunate was abolished,
and political power was returned to the Emperor.

The Meiji Era, which began after the Boshin War, was
characterized by a series of political, social, and economic
reforms that modernized Japan and turned it into a world
power in the 20th century.

71

The Bakumatsu was a period in Japanese history that spanned from the late 18th century to the mid-19th century.

This period was marked by a series of social, political, and economic changes that laid the groundwork for the modernization of Japan and the end of the Tokugawa Shogunate.

The term Bakumatsu means 'end of the bakufu,' which was the feudal political system in power in Japan during that time.

The Tokugawa Shogunate, headed by the shogun, had governed Japan since the 17th century and was based on a system of political and military control by the feudal lords, or daimyos.

During the Bakumatsu, Japan experienced a series of significant changes, including the forced opening of the country to foreign trade with the West, the arrival of new technologies, and increasing popular discontent with the Shogunate government.

These changes led to a series of conflicts, both internal and external, which ultimately resulted in the end of the Shogunate and the beginning of the Meiji Era.

Among the most notable events of the Bakumatsu were the arrival of the 'Black Ships' from the United States led by Matthew Perry, the Namamugi Incident in which a daimyo attacked British citizens, the previously mentioned Boshin War, and the Meiji Restoration that led to the end of the Tokugawa Shogunate and the beginning of the Meiji Era.

72

Toyotomi Hideyoshi was a military and political leader who unified Japan in the late 16th century.

Hideyoshi began his career as a simple soldier serving Oda Nobunaga, a daimyo who was attempting to unify Japan under his rule.

After Nobunaga's death in 1582, Hideyoshi continued his work and ultimately succeeded in reunifying Japan in 1590.

Hideyoshi implemented a series of structural reforms to stabilize the country and strengthen his position as leader.

This included land redistribution, the abolition of the feudal system of vassalage, and the promotion of agriculture and trade.

He also established a centralized control system that allowed him to effectively govern all of Japan's territory.

Hideyoshi is also known for his policies of pacification and promotion of culture.

For example, he prohibited the carrying of weapons among the civilian population and ordered the construction of the famous Osaka Castle as a demonstration of power and stability in Japan.

He also encouraged art and literature, including the development of Noh theater.

Although Hideyoshi was a unifier of Japan, his reign was brief.

After his death in 1598, a power struggle erupted among his successors, which eventually led to the civil war known as the Battle of Sekigahara in 1600.

This battle consolidated the power of the Tokugawa clan and marked the beginning of the Edo period in Japanese history.

73

The diet of the samurai varied depending on the era and their social status.

During the early years of the Japanese feudal period, samurai were often farmers who lived off the land.

The basic food of the samurai consisted of rice, miso soup, and a variety of seasonal vegetables and fruits.

They also consumed animal protein in the form of fish, seafood, poultry, and beef or pork on special occasions.

However, meat was not an integral part of the samurai diet, as it was not easily available in large quantities.

Samurai also consumed a drink called 'sake,' which is a type of fermented rice wine.

This beverage played an important role in samurai culture and was consumed during ceremonies and rituals, as well as with meals.

In addition to their diet, samurai also practiced a type of etiquette called 'samurai-dō,' which included rules for eating.

For example, samurai ate from shallow bowls to prevent hiding weapons in their food and drank from small cups to avoid intoxication and remain alert.

74

During the Heian period (794-1185), aristocrats and members of the upper classes slept in beds made of several tatami mats stacked on top of each other, known as yaedatami.

The number of layers used was proportional to the person's rank.

Samurai, on the other hand, had a different way of sleeping.

Samurai often slept on thin mattresses called 'futons' that were placed directly on the tatami floor in a room known as 'washitsu.'

These rooms were designed to be multifunctional, used for both sleeping, receiving visitors, and eating.

Futons were rolled up and stored in closets during the day so that the space could be used for other purposes.

Additionally, samurai often shared the room with other family members or servants, so several futons were laid out on the floor.

Samurai also had a practice called 'yagura-kakushi,' which involved hiding in small holes in the wall at night to be alert in case of an enemy attack.

These holes were often located behind paintings or in false walls in the room.

75

Samurai houses varied in size and design depending on their social position and wealth, as well as the historical period in which they lived.

However, there are some common characteristics that can be identified.

In general, samurai houses were made of wood and built in a traditional Japanese style.

They had sloping roofs covered with straw or ceramic tiles and were raised off the ground on columns.

The height of the houses depended on the social status of the owner, with higher-ranking samurai having taller houses.

The houses were divided into rooms by sliding paper or wood panels called 'shoji' and 'fusuma,' which allowed for the creation of different spaces according to the residents' needs.

Samurai houses also typically featured traditional Japanese gardens, with ponds and stone bridges, and some had their own dojo or martial arts training space.

Regarding the internal layout, the houses usually had a main entrance that led to a central hall or corridor called 'genkan.'

From here, one could access different rooms, such as the kitchen, dining room, family members' bedrooms, and spaces for receiving visitors.

Samurai houses in rural areas tended to be single-story, with hardened earth floors (doma) where cooking and other daily activities took place, and a raised wooden-floored area for sleeping.

76

**Minamoto no Tametomo:
One of the most skilled archers in history.**

In multiple stories, it is claimed that the samurai Minamoto no Tametomo was born with a deformity where one of his arms was several centimeters longer than the other.

Supposedly, this genetic anomaly allowed him to execute more powerful bow shots than any other warrior in history.

Legend has it that when mounted on a horse, he was virtually unbeatable.

During the centuries he was active, Minamoto no Tametomo became a symbol of strength and destruction among samurai warriors.

Among his many feats, there is a legend that claims he once sank a ship of the Taira clan with a single arrow, directing the projectile to an area just below the waterline.

On his return journey to Japan, Minamoto no Tametomo faced superior forces and never surrendered.

He never allowed himself to be captured and ultimately died by seppuku, refusing all the time to fall into enemy hands.

77

Miyamoto Musashi: the swordsman who invented a battle style.

In 1595, Miyamoto Musashi killed his first opponent, a samurai from a neighboring village, when he was just 13 years old.

Legend has it that Musashi was armed only with a wooden training sword, but that was enough to defeat his opponent in less than a minute.

He threw the samurai to the ground and struck his throat so hard that, supposedly, he died choking on his own blood.

From that moment, Musashi began an extensive journey across Japan seeking to become the greatest swordsman of his time, and he succeeded.

Before reaching the age of 20, he had fiercely fought in multiple battles, emerging unscathed from all of them.

He then inaugurated the tradition of traveling the country to seek and kill anyone who considered themselves a master swordsman.

In multiple duels, Miyamoto Musashi destroyed a famous clan of swordsmen from the Yoshioka family.

During the same period, the samurai began wielding two swords in combat, a technique completely unknown in the world of the samurai.

By 1613, Musashi had established himself as a true warrior, defeating some of the most famous duelists in Japan.

However, he eventually met Sasaki Kojiro, one of the most formidable opponents in his entire career.

From that moment on, Musashi swore that he would only fight duels to the death.

He continued accumulating victories until 1645, when he began to feel his end was near.

Instead of sitting and waiting for death, Musashi isolated himself in a cave where he wrote 'The Book of Five Rings,' detailing the classic swordplay of Japan with precision, and also wrote a guide on self-reliance called 'Dokkodo'.

78

Tomoe Gozen was a legendary warrior in Japanese history, known for her swordsmanship skills and bravery on the battlefield.

Her story dates back to the 12th century, during the era of the samurai.

It is said that Tomoe Gozen was the concubine of Minamoto no Yoshinaka, a famous daimyo and samurai general.

Although women were not typically warriors in the Japanese society of that time, Tomoe Gozen was an exception, as she was reportedly a skilled archer and expert in longsword handling.

Tomoe Gozen's fame as a warrior began to spread after a battle in which she participated alongside Yoshinaka against a rival daimyo.

On that occasion, she is said to have fought with great bravery and skill, and was able to defeat several enemies.

However, the most famous moment of Tomoe Gozen's career as a warrior came in 1181, during the Battle of Yokotagawara.

In that battle, she is said to have fought against seven enemy warriors at the same time, defeating them all, beheading them, and carrying their heads as trophies to her home.

In the Battle of Uchide no Hama in 1184, Tomoe Gozen led a group of 300 men against a much larger enemy army of 6,000 soldiers.

Despite the numerical disadvantage, Tomoe Gozen and her men fought with great bravery and skill, inflicting significant losses on the enemy.

After the death of Yoshinaka, Tomoe Gozen disappears from historical records, and her fate remains unknown.

However, her legacy as one of the few female samurai warriors of her time continues to be remembered in Japanese culture to this day.

79

In the era of the samurai, there was a class of people known as 'miko' or 'onmyoji,' who were considered sorcerers or magicians in Japanese culture.

These individuals were known for their abilities to predict the future, perform rituals and spells for protection or to invoke spirits, and they were also said to be able to control the weather and other natural phenomena.

Onmyoji often worked for the imperial court and nobles, and they were believed to possess great power and knowledge that enabled them to influence significant events and decisions.

Some of the most famous onmyoji include Abe no Seimei and Kamo no Yasunori, who lived during the Heian era in the 10th century.

It was said that onmyoji lived in sacred places like shrines, temples, and mountains, where they could connect with spirits and gods.

These places were also believed to have special energy that could be harnessed by onmyoji for their rituals and spells.

Regarding their powers, onmyoji were said to be able to communicate with the spirits of the dead, perform rituals to invoke the protection of the gods, and use magic to influence people's luck and destiny.

They were also believed to control natural elements like wind and rain, and to predict the future through astrology and other divination methods.

As for stories, there are many legends about onmyoji in Japanese literature and popular culture.

One of the most famous is the story of Abe no Seimei, who was said to have the power to control demons and evil spirits.

The character of Minamoto no Hiromasa in the folk tale 'The Three-legged Crow' is also believed to be an onmyoji who had the ability to read the future through bird watching.

80

During the late 9th and early 10th centuries, Japan faced a series of crises that led to popular revolts and political and social instability in the country.

These crises were largely caused by periods of famine and plagues that affected the population, as well as by the weakness of the central government and the corruption of officials.

Faced with a lack of resources and the inability to handle the revolts, the central government was forced to rely on feudal lords or daimyos to provide military troops to confront the rebellions.

This led to the daimyos starting to play an increasingly important role in Japanese politics and society.

The growing military influence of the daimyos was due in part to their ability to recruit and train their own troops, and also to their ability to maintain order in their territories.

Over time, the daimyos began to accumulate more power and wealth, becoming true feudal lords with their own army and administration.

This process of militarization also had significant cultural and social consequences in Japan.

On the one hand, there was a rise in bushido, the ethical code of the samurai, which emphasized loyalty, honor, and bravery in battle.

On the other hand, the increasing militarization of Japanese society also led to the construction of castles, fortifications, and other military engineering works, as well as the proliferation of advanced weapons and armor.

81

The period known as the Sengoku Jidai, or Era of the Warring States, began in Japan in the 15th century and lasted until the end of the 16th century.

This era was characterized by the collapse of central power and the fragmentation of the country into small feudal states known as han.

During this period, there was constant struggle among daimyos, feudal lords who ruled their own territories with their own armies, to gain absolute control of the country.

The era of the Warring States originated largely due to the weakness of the central government and the inability of the emperors and shoguns to maintain control over the daimyos and samurai.

This situation led to an increase in the power and influence of the daimyos, who became the true rulers of their territories.

One of the most famous conflicts of the Warring States Era was the Genpei War, a conflict that lasted five years (1180-1185) and pitted two powerful clans against each other: the Minamoto and the Taira.

The Genpei War was a bloody conflict that involved numerous battles and skirmishes throughout the country, having a significant impact on Japan's history and culture.

During the Genpei War, samurai played an indispensable role in each battle serving their lords, the daimyos.

Samurai were warriors trained in martial arts and advanced military tactics, and were considered the most skilled and brave warriors of the time.

In battles, samurai fought hand-to-hand with swords and bows, and their skill and courage were fundamental to the victory of their armies.

82

Samurai were not just the elite.

Many people believe that samurai were a fighting force composed of the Japanese elite, but the truth is that most of the army was made up of infantry soldiers, known as Ashigaru.

These were individuals who started from the bottom, emerging from labor in rice plantations.

However, the landowners, known as daimyo, noticed their skills and trained them for combat.

Japan had three types of warriors: samurai, Ashigaru, and ji-samurai.

These were people who worked in the fields most of the time, serving as samurai on certain occasions, similar to army reservists.

There was a hierarchy among them, so warriors could advance in rank; for example, a ji-samurai could assume the position of a full-time samurai and join the group.

Ashigaru were not as respected as the samurai.

In some parts of Japan, the two classes of warriors were barely distinguishable as they assumed similar responsibilities and duties.

83

Christian Samurai.

When Jesuits arrived in southern Japan, some daimyo knights converted to Christianity, but most did so for pragmatic reasons, as conversion granted them access to European military technology.

For example, Arima Harunobu, a Christian daimyo, used European weapons in his battle at Okita-Nawate.

By converting to Christianity, another daimyo, known as Dom Justo Takayama, found it challenging to act as any other samurai warrior during his reign.

When Japan expelled the missionaries, it forced Japanese Christians to renounce Christianity.

Takayama, however, chose to flee with 300 followers rather than renounce his faith.

84

The idea of retreating from battles was considered shameful by samurai, as they were expected to fight to the death to demonstrate their loyalty and bravery.

The concept of 'seppuku,' or ritual suicide, was a way to avoid dishonor, as samurai preferred to die by their own hand rather than fall into enemy hands.

However, in some situations, daimyos considered the withdrawal of the army as a strategic option to save lives and resources.

This practice was common in Japan and elsewhere and was often used to lure the enemy into an ambush.

The samurai of the Shimazu clan, from southern Japan, were known for their skills in guerrilla warfare and for using false retreat tactics to draw the enemy into positions where they could be attacked more effectively.

In general, the decision to retreat from a battle was difficult and was considered a last resort to avoid total defeat.

85

Kamo no Yasunori was a famous onmyoji, or Japanese magician, who lived during the 9th century in the imperial court of Kyoto.

The practice of onmyodo focused on astrology, divination, and magic, and was considered a very important spiritual discipline in the imperial court at the time.

Kamo no Yasunori was a member of the Kamo clan, which was responsible for religious rituals at the Kamo Shrine in Kyoto.

As an onmyoji, he was known for his skill in divination and in using magic to influence the political and military events of the era.

It is said that Kamo no Yasunori had a significant influence on the lives of several emperors, including Emperor Uda and Emperor Daigo.

He is also credited with various powerful rituals and spells, such as using a magical mirror to repel an attack by pirates from Tsushima in 894.

Kamo no Yasunori also authored several books on onmyodo, including 'Yume no Kuni no Tsurugi' (The Sword of the Country of Dreams), which is considered one of the most important treatises on Japanese magic.

Although the practice of onmyodo declined in importance after the Heian period, Kamo no Yasunori is remembered as one of the most significant onmyoji in Japanese history.

86

Abe no Seimei was one of the most famous onmyoji in Japanese history, living during the Heian period in the 10th century.

As an onmyoji, he specialized in astrology, divination, and magic, and his skill in these practices earned him great fame and reputation at the imperial court in Kyoto.

According to legend, Abe no Seimei was born from a relationship between a woman and a demon.

From an early age, he showed supernatural abilities, and his father, who turned out to be an onmyoji, taught him everything he knew about magic and divination.

As an adult, Abe no Seimei became the most famous onmyoji of his time, working as an advisor to the emperors of the time.

It is said that Abe no Seimei had the ability to see and communicate with spirits, and that he could also foresee the future and perform powerful spells.

Some of his most famous abilities include the ability to invoke natural elements and heal diseases.

In addition to his supernatural abilities, Abe no Seimei was also known for his skill as an astronomer and mathematician, and he is credited with several inventions and discoveries in these areas.

Abe no Seimei has become a very popular character in Japanese culture, and has been portrayed in literary, theatrical, and film works.

He is considered one of the most important onmyoji in Japanese history, and his legacy has endured to this day.

87

The theory that samurais might descend from the Ainu ethnic group is a possibility raised by some historians and anthropologists.

The Ainu are an indigenous ethnic group that historically inhabited the island of Hokkaido, as well as parts of Honshu Island and Sakhalin.

Unlike the Japanese, the Ainu had a different physical appearance, including lighter skin and abundant, wavy hair.

However, this theory is only speculative and there is no conclusive evidence to support it.

Moreover, the samurais were a very diverse social group, composed of people from different ethnic backgrounds, not just Japanese.

The rigorous martial training and possession of weapons are not necessarily related to perceptions of racial purity.

It is important to highlight that discrimination against the Ainu and other ethnic groups in Japan has been a historical issue, and although there have been advances to combat this prejudice, discrimination still exists today.

88

In Japanese feudal society, arranged marriages were very common, and samurais were no exception.

Marriage was seen as an alliance between two families, and therefore, it was not just a matter of love or attraction, but a strategic decision.

High-ranking samurais often married women from families of equal or higher status, which ensured an even higher social and economic position for them.

Meanwhile, lower-ranking samurais often married women from their own class or the lower class, such as commoners or peasants, which allowed them to improve their social standing.

In these marriages, the woman's family had to provide a dowry consisting of material goods, such as land, money, or, in some cases, food.

The tradition of giving a ton of sushi as part of the dowry is an example of the importance given to food in Japanese culture.

Overall, marriages were a matter of strategy and alliance, and although there were exceptions, love and attraction were not the main considerations.

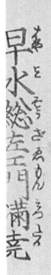

89

Divorce in samurai culture was allowed, but it was uncommon and frowned upon.

Society greatly valued family stability and marital fidelity.

In the event that a samurai wanted to divorce, he had to return the dowry to his wife's family.

If the marriage had been arranged by a third party, this third party could also be affected in their reputation, as they were supposed to have made a good choice in the marriage and guaranteed the stability and happiness of the couple.

In some cases, samurais could resort to separation instead of divorce, which meant that the couple lived apart, but were not considered legally divorced.

This was an option for cases where the couple could no longer cohabit, but did not want to face the social stigma of divorce.

90

Honda Tadakatsu (1548 – 1610).

Skilled in the use of various weapons, the favorite weapon of this Japanese warrior was the tonbo-giri spear, one of the three most lethal Japanese spears, with an extremely fine and sharp tip.

He was known on the battlefield for wearing very light armor that allowed him total freedom of movement, matched with a helmet adorned with deer antlers.

This warrior of ancient Japan fought in the late 16th century, a time when the samurais lost the glory they had in previous centuries.

However, he managed to honor his profession, becoming one of the most remembered historical warriors in legends.

Many stories are told of Tadakatsu, such as the one that says he overcame more than 100 battles without having suffered a single wound or scratch.

He is known as the warrior who surpassed death, although this may be due to the great admiration he received from both his lords and his enemies.

He worked under the orders of ruler Tokugawa Ieyasu, fighting until the beginning of the Edo period, which allowed for more information about his feats.

He was one of the great generals of his army, sometimes taking the front in battle in place of his superiors, always accompanied by his horse Mikuniguro.

Toyotomi Hideyoshi (1536 – 1598).

Alongside Oda Nobunaga and Tokugawa Ieyasu, Toyotomi Hideyoshi was one of the samurai warriors who belonged to the "three great unifiers of Japan."

He was a fighter who did not come from any significant clan or even a noble family.

He rose from a lower caste to become the trusted man of Oda Nobunaga, standing out above the rest of the generals.

He proclaimed himself as "the Taiko," a title very well received by his followers.

Starting at the lowest rank in the army, as an ashigaru, he earned the respect of his superiors and lords, as well as the fear of his enemies on the battlefield.

From his warrior origins, his rise to power led him to participate in political decisions.

He proposed political reforms that laid the groundwork for the subsequent Tokugawa shogunate in the 17th century.

He transitioned from the battlefield to a diplomatic position in just a few years, although he never completely abandoned his combat training.

In the mid-16th century, Hideyoshi married a young woman from an aristocratic family and continued working as a military strategist.

Through bribes and favors, he managed to separate and defeat various enemy clans, demonstrating that a samurai's worth is not always shown in his skill with the bow or sword.

92

Takeda Shingen (1521 – 1573).

He was one of the greatest warriors in the history of Japan, who participated in the battles for control of the empire during the Sengoku period.

He was known as "the Tiger of Kai," and his greatest rival on the battlefield, Uesugi Kenshin, was "the Dragon of Echigo," two enemy animals also in Buddhist mythology.

The young Shingen was born as the son of the chief of the Takeda clan, which granted him from an early age the great honor of receiving the best training with different weapons.

This status was also reflected in his life in the quality and type of armor he used, with extraordinary decorations that distinguished him from the rest of the army leaders.

His constant disputes with his father in his youth led him to wrest control of the clan from him, putting him at the head through a series of victories, most against the rival Uesugi clan.

It was against this army that the Takeda clan was finally eliminated, losing control for many years.

After the leader's death, his son Takeda Katsuyori took over as the clan chief, attempting to raise his family's glory once again.

It was not until generations later that they regained the importance they once had, with a combative leader like the famous samurai Takeda Shingen once was.

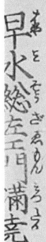

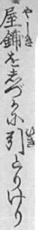

93

Minamoto Yoshitsune (1159 – 1189).

A member of the Minamoto clan, he fought alongside Gozen in the Genpei Wars.

He became one of the clan's great leaders when part of his family died during the Heiji Rebellion, and some of his brothers were exiled.

During his childhood, he was cared for by monks north of Kyoto, before joining the armies initially with the Taira clan.

He started by winning several battles, which allowed him to quickly rise in rank.

This restored honor to his family, recovering after the failures that had sidelined them.

Yoshitsune elevated his surname once again, making it the dominant clan in the country.

His role in each of the battles he participated in was primarily as a commander, mobilizing troops.

More than a feared warrior, he was one of the best samurai strategists in history, though he always maintained his position with his sword in the front line in combat, showing great bravery.

After the war, he was pursued by his brother Yoritomo, who ended his life at only 30 years old.

Many legends about his tragic death exist today, forming part of Japanese folklore.

The figures of both warriors appear in many series, movies, and even video games.

94

Date Masamune (1566 — 1636).

Masamune participated in the military conflicts that took place in Japan just before the beginning of the Edo Period.

He lived between the 16th and 17th centuries, descending from a noble family from which he learned to lead both on and off the battlefield.

At just 14 years old, he began assisting his father in leading his first military campaign.

At the age of 17, he took command of his army, conquering much of the country, and joining forces with other lords from different clans to fight against the enemy.

He was always surrounded by military men twice his age, proving himself to be a very advanced youth in war tactics, both in battle and siege.

A distinguishing feature was that he always wore a bell-shaped helmet with a large crescent moon on the top.

He was known as "the one-eyed dragon," because, curiously, he lost sight in his right eye due to smallpox as a child, although this did not prevent him from having the best vision for conquest.

In addition to building many palaces in the region he reigned over and founding the city of Sendai, he also focused on sending ships to distant lands.

He was one of the pioneers in introducing Christianity to Japan, as well as culture from Europe and Colonial America of the time.

95

Oda Nobunaga (1534 – 1582).

The son of a minor lord, Oda Nobunaga rose to become a daimyo, or Japanese feudal lord, of great significance through his own merits.

His family was divided in the mid-16th century, and after his father's death, he fought against other members to take control, even confronting his own brother.

This decisiveness characterized his entire military career.

From the start of his rule, he founded a small army with only 3,000 soldiers, with whom he began to conquer large territories.

His swordsmanship and military strategies were his best weapons.

Though not very well-known in the rest of the world, in Japan, he is one of the most famous samurais because he was one of the precursors of the unification of the different territories of the country, restoring its former status as an Empire.

He led the ancient city of Kyoto alongside his vassals, with a great sense of honor that was even praised by his enemies.

However, it was honor that led to his demise, resulting in suicide.

When his most trusted general, Akechi Mitsuhide, betrayed him, he set fire to the temple where Nobunaga was living, and then took his own life using the solemn technique of harakiri.

96

Hojo Masako (1157 – 1225).

A Japanese warrior of great beauty and a political leader of the country's major regions from the late 12th to the early 13th century, she fought alongside the Minamoto clan, establishing the shogunate.

This onna bugeisha, or female warrior, was trained by her own father from childhood.

She learned horseback riding, the art of traditional hunting and fishing, the use of the katana, the long Japanese saber or naginata, and other traditional weapons.

She also had the honor of participating with her father in political decisions and military strategies, acquiring a leadership character that made her stand out above other men in the clan.

Masako was a very calculating and strategic female samurai, both in battle and in politics.

This led her to conquer much of Japan's lands, leading her army alongside Minamoto no Yoritomo, her right-hand man, against the Taira clan.

Hojo Masako is one of the most important samurais in Japan because she was the first woman in command, with a power that no other military woman has had since.

Together with Yoritomo and Tokimasa, both brothers from the Minamoto clan, she shared absolute power in the country for many years.

97

Ishida Mitsunari (1559 – November 6, 1600).

He was a Japanese samurai who commanded the Western Army at the Battle of Sekigahara during the Azuchi-Momoyama period of the 16th century.

Mitsunari was born in the southern part of Ōmi Province (now Shiga Prefecture) and was the second son of Ishida Masatsugu, who was a commander serving the Azai clan, which they abandoned after their defeat in 1573.

When Hideyoshi led campaigns in the Chūgoku region, Mitsunari was involved in attacks on castles such as Tottori Castle and Takamatsu Castle.

As Hideyoshi gained significant political power in the country, Mitsunari was recognized as a talented financial administrator due to his knowledge and skill in calculations.

From 1585, Mitsunari became the administrator of Sakai Province, a position he held alongside his older brother, Ishida Masazumi.

Mitsunari was chosen as one of the five bugyo or senior administrators of Hideyoshi's government, who appointed him daimyo of Sawayama in Ōmi Province, granting him an estate of 500,000 koku.

Mitsunari was the leader of the bureaucrats in Hideyoshi's government and was known for his strict character.

Although he had many friends, he was at odds with some renowned daimyo who were good warriors, including Fukushima Masanori, a relative of Hideyoshi.

The central point of the conflict was the question of whether Tokugawa Ieyasu could be trusted to support the Toyotomi government, given that the successor, Toyotomi Hideyori, was only a child.

In 1600, the Battle of Sekigahara occurred as a result of this political conflict.

Mitsunari succeeded in organizing an army commanded by Mori Terumoto, but the coalition led by Tokugawa Ieyasu was larger, resulting in Mitsunari's defeat.

Although he tried to escape, he was captured by some villagers.

He was taken to the Rokujō ga hara execution grounds in Kyoto, where he was beheaded with a single sword stroke, alongside other Western Army daimyo like Konishi Yukinaga and Ankokuji Ekei.

His head was displayed in Kyoto for a time for passersby to see.

98

Kusunoki Masashige (1294 – July 4, 1336).

He was a samurai landowner from Kawachi Province.

In 1331, he fought in support of Emperor Go-Daigo as part of the plan to remove the leadership of Japan from the Kamakura Shogunate and is remembered as the ideal of samurai loyalty.

In his first mission, commanding 500 men, he was joined by Prince Moriyoshi.

When Emperor Go-Daigo was captured, Kusunoki Masashige and Prince Morinaga remained loyal to him and continued the rebellion.

In a three-week battle, they defended Akasaka and Mount Kongō, even though they were outnumbered and the shogun's men cut off their water supply.

Eventually, Kusunoki ordered the castle to be burned and fled, making the Hojo believe he had committed suicide.

The following year, Kusunoki gathered more men and began fighting against the Kamakura Shogunate's troops in Kinai, while Prince Moriyoshi persuaded other warriors and landowners to join against Kamakura.

In 1333, due to the easy fall of Akasaka and Yoshino castles, Kusunoki prepared Chihaya Castle, where he was located, for a long battle against a considerable number of men the shogun sent against Chihaya.

In this battle, he used everything from rolling logs to boiling water, holding out until Ashikaga Takauji and his army took and occupied Kyoto in the name of Emperor Go-Daigo.

In 1336, Ashikaga Takauji turned away from the imperial cause.

By order of the emperor, and loyal to him, Kusunoki Masashige summoned his army, knowing they were doomed to die.

Kusunoki and his troops settled on the Minatogawa River, on its western bank, accompanied by Nitta Yoshisada (the emperor's main commander) and his troops on the river's eastern bank.

After a six-hour battle (Battle of Minatogawa), Kusunoki Masashige, his brother Kusunoki Masanori, and some of his vassals committed suicide.

Years after his death, following the Meiji Restoration, Kusunoki Masashige became a national symbol for his unwavering loyalty to the emperor until his death.

One of his famous quotes was: "Injustice does not conquer principles, principles do not conquer the law, the law does not conquer power, power does not conquer heaven."

99

Akechi Mitsuhide (明智 光秀, 1528 – July 2, 1582).

He was a Japanese samurai who lived during the Sengoku Period, also known by the nicknames Jūbei or Koretō Hyūga no Kami.

He was a general under the command of daimyo Oda Nobunaga, whom he later betrayed, forcing him to commit seppuku.

Mitsuhide was born in Mino Province (now Gifu Prefecture) and was a descendant of the Toki clan.

He began serving Nobunaga after the conquest of Mino Province in 1566, receiving Sakamoto in Ōmi Province in 1571, which was valued at 100,000 koku, thereby becoming a daimyo himself.

In 1579, he captured Yakami Castle, controlled by Hatano Hideharu, promising him terms of peace, but Nobunaga did not fulfill them and ordered Hideharu's execution.

The execution of Hideharu offended members of the Hatano clan, leading some of them to kill Mitsuhide's mother.

The situation worsened when Nobunaga publicly insulted Mitsuhide, which even caught the attention of some foreign observers.

Mitsuhide blamed Nobunaga for his mother's death, thus fulfilling his revenge with the "Incident at Honnōji" on June 21, 1582.

Although Mitsuhide did not personally kill Nobunaga, as is commonly attributed, he did force him to commit seppuku.

Upon hearing of the events, both Hideyoshi Toyotomi and Ieyasu Tokugawa rushed to avenge Nobunaga and take his place.

Hideyoshi found Mitsuhide first, and although Mitsuhide survived for 14 days, he was ultimately defeated along with his allies at the Battle of Yamazaki.

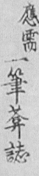

100

Sanada Saemon-no-Suke Nobushige (1567 – June 3, 1615).

He was a Japanese samurai, the second son of Sengoku period daimyo Sanada Masayuki.

He received several titles throughout his life, such as "Hero who appears only once every hundred years," "Crimson Demon of War," and "The Number One Warrior in Japan."

During the Battle of Nagashino, Masayuki's two older brothers, who served the Takeda clan, were killed, leading him to inherit the leadership of the clan and occupy Ueda Castle.

In 1582, the combined forces of the Oda clan, led by Oda Nobunaga, and the Tokugawa clan, led by Tokugawa Ieyasu, destroyed the Takeda clan.

The Sanada clan initially surrendered under Nobunaga's orders, but after the Honnō-ji Incident, where Nobunaga was betrayed and forced to commit seppuku by one of his main generals, Akechi Mitsuhide, they regained their independence and served under various powerful daimyo such as the Uesugi clan, the late Hōjō clan, and the Tokugawa clan.

In 1600, Tokugawa Ieyasu summoned various daimyo to attack Uesugi Kagekatsu, so the Sanada joined in.

However, when Ishida Mitsunari decided to confront Ieyasu in combat, Masayuki and Nobushige joined him, while Nobushige's brother, Nobuyuki, joined Ieyasu's army.

The Sanada retreated to Ueda Castle, and when Tokugawa Hidetada marched on the Nakasendō, the Sanada forced Hidetada's 40,000-man army to retreat with just 2,000 men.

Realizing the extra effort needed to besiege the castle, Hidetada withdrew but failed to arrive at the Battle of Sekigahara in time.

After the war, Ieyasu wanted to execute the Sanada, but due to Nobuyuki's contributions to his cause, their lives were spared, and they were exiled to Kudoyama in Kii Province, where Masayuki died.

12 years later, relations between the Toyotomi clan and Ieyasu deteriorated, prompting the Toyotomi clan to start recruiting ronin to prepare for war.

Nobushige escaped from Kudoyama and entered Osaka Castle to fight as well.

During the Siege of Osaka, Nobushige built fortifications along the southern part of the castle at its weakest points, from which he launched attacks against Ieyasu's army with groups of 6,000 arquebusiers.

Outnumbered, Nobushige's forces were defeated, and he lost his life at the age of 49, giving rise to the legend that would form over the years.

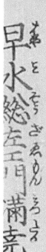

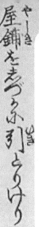

101

Nakano Takeko (中野 竹子, Edo, April 1847 – October 10, 1868).

She was a female samurai from the Aizu domain who fought and died in the Boshin War.

She was the daughter of Nakano Heinai, an Aizu official.

She was intensely trained in martial arts and educated in literature, and was adopted by her teacher Akaoka Daisuke.

She served as a martial arts instructor along with her adoptive father from the early 1860s.

During the Battle of Aizu, she stepped forward to defend Wakamatsu Castle with her naginata and a corps of female fighters who were not officially part of the domain's military forces.

Initially, the commanders were reluctant to accept the group of women, but they agreed due to Takeko's insistence.

It is said she even threatened to commit suicide if they were not allowed to participate in the castle's defense.

This unit was later called the Women's Army (娘子隊 Jōshitai).

Her unit led the defense against the Imperial Japanese Army with troops from the Ōgaki domain in the Battle of Wakamatsu Castle, where she was shot in the chest on October 10, 1868.

To avoid the dishonor of being captured by her enemies, 21-year-old Takeko asked her younger sister, Yūko, to behead her.

Her sister brought her head to the Hōkaiji temple (currently in Aizubange, Fukushima) where it was buried under a pine tree.

In the same temple, there is an altar in her honor where her naginata is kept.

If you have enjoyed the content of this book about samurais, we would love to invite you to leave a review on Amazon.

Your opinion is very valuable to us and to other readers seeking accurate and entertaining information about samurai culture.

Additionally, your review will help us improve our work and continue creating quality content for lovers of history and Japanese culture.

We understand that leaving a review can be a tedious process, but we appreciate you taking a few minutes of your time to share your thoughts and opinions with us.

Your support is crucial to us and motivates us to continue working to offer you interesting content about samurai culture.

Thank you very much for your support.

May the gods of war accompany you on your path and protect you from any danger!

★ ★ ★ ★ ★